the Flame of Incarnation

David Spangler

Essays

Books by David Spangler

The Call

Blessing: *The Art and the Practice*

Parent as Mystic - Mystic as Parent

Manifestation: *Creating the life you love*

Everyday Miracles

The Story Tree

The Incarnational Card Deck and Manual

Incarnational Spirituality: *A strategy to bless our World*

World Work: *Inner Activism*

Crafting Home: *Generating the Sacred*

Crafting Relationships: *The Holding of Others*

Engaging the Subtle Worlds: *The Incarnational Way*

Acknowledgements

This book grows from a series of electronic essays written monthly and sent to those who have signed up for what I call "David's Desk" distributed through the Lorian Association.

Thanks to all who have honored me with taking the time to open Lorian's email newsletters, read the essays, respond with comments and occasionally forward them on to friends. Your attention is greatly appreciated.

If you have seen one or more of these essays previously online I hope you enjoy revisiting them here in this book format. If not, and you like what you read, you can sign up to receive future free online essays at www.Lorian.org.

The Flame of Incarnation

Copyright © 2009 David Spangler

All rights reserved, including the right to reproduce this book, or portions thereof, in any form.

Edited by Julia Spangler

Cover Art by Deborah Koff-Chapin
www.touchdrawing.com

Published by Lorian Press
2204 E Grand Ave., Everett, WA 98201

ISBN 10: 0-936878-27-4
ISBN 13: 978-0-936878-27-0

Spangler/David
The Flame of Incarnation/David Spangler

First Edition: June 2009

Printed in the United States of America
0 9 8 7 6 5 4 3 2 1

www.lorian.org

Contents

The Flame of Incarnation 1
Spirituality in Everyday Life 5
Thresholds 11
Surviving in Hard Times 17
Living the Times 33
Spiritual Energy 41
Decisions 47
No Muggles Here! 53
Language 61
Ego 69
The Haggled Self 77
The Sweet Spot 83
The Incarnational Way 91

The Flame of Incarnation

Introduction

The idea of incarnation has such a feeling of solidity and density about it. The roots of the word itself mean to take on or enter into flesh, literally to become meat. Thinking about this, one cannot help but feel as if something ephemeral, sparkling and free—our spirit—is being closed in, captured, and bound in a cave of protoplasm. How awful! No wonder our physical life is so often perceived as a kind of imprisonment, our souls bound to a world of flesh and matter from which we seek release.

This idea that incarnation is a loss of something and that physical life is a fallen, limited state pervades many of our spiritual and philosophical traditions in one form or another and affects our behavior upon the earth. At worst it leads us to devalue physical life and the physical world. Why appreciate a place that imprisons us? We want to survive it. We want to get through it with as little pain and suffering as possible. If we end up trashing the world in the process, well, it's not our real home anyway.

It is hyperbole to suggest that this idea is at the root of all that is wrong with our world and all the suffering of humanity. But it can be said with justification that attitudes that devalue the physical body, nature, our personalities, and the incarnate state don't help. Particularly in our time when we face global challenges of environmental degradation and climate change and when our ability to kill each other many times over (and destroy much of the ecology with us) is not matched by our empathy and compassion, any ideas or attitudes that diminish our capacity and willingness to love ourselves, each other and the world we inhabit are less than useless. They are dangerous. They are potentially fatal.

For this reason a spirituality that celebrates and appreciates incarnation and that understands its sacred roots is timely. It can lead us to rethink and reimagine who we are and what our relationship is to the earth and to the sacred. It can uncover spiritual resources within us that we might otherwise overlook because we don't expect to find them in our incarnate state. Such a spirituality might lead us to learn how to "think like a planet," how to honor ourselves and each other in new ways, and how to hold our world and each other in greater love and wholeness.

Such a spirituality is timely as well because our understanding of ourselves and of our world has changed and is changing in profound ways, largely due to the investigations and discoveries of physics, biology, neuroscience, and the holistic sciences of complexity and systems theory. Matter is no longer conceived of as dense, hard, static, and unyielding. Instead, it is seen as energy in motion, dancing and vibrant. The flesh that clothes us is less a prison than a complex melody, a song of collaboration and life, change and emergence.

Many years ago I taught a series of workshops and classes I collectively called "Journey into Fire." The underlying concept was that within us each was a dynamic presence of creative consciousness and energy, a flame of being and sacredness emanating life and love into the cosmos. We were each miniature stars, generative and radiant. The purpose of the classes was to explore ways to tap and unleash this inner fire in creative ways in our lives. But as I pursued this image, I began to see that it was incomplete. It veered too closely to what could be called the "M & M theory of incarnation:" having a sweet desirable center surrounded by a hard, protective exterior. It was not the incarnational spirituality that I wanted to explore and present.

But seeing the physical world as radiant energy, as a spiritual "fire" in its own right, shifted my perspective. Incarnation became for me not the entry of a flame into a container that could hold it, like placing a lit candle into a lantern, but rather two distinct fires blending and merging with each other, each drawing on the inexhaustible kindling of the Sacred, each adding to each other's radiance and power, creating together an emergent flame of incarnation. Rather than being imprisoned, the soul is expanded in its engagement with matter and the world, giving it the place and opportunity to express the love at the heart of its existence. From this image of partnership (and a lot of inner research and contemplative inquiry) Incarnational Spirituality has emerged.

This emergence has largely been mediated through online classes producing hundreds of pages of text exploring many aspects of this incarnational spirituality. It has developed a cosmology as well as exercises and practices for making its insights practical within our daily lives. Slowly, this information is finding its way into books and other media so that it can be accessible. (You can see what's already available by visiting our website, www.Lorian.org.) At heart, though, incarnational spirituality is an attitude, a way of seeing ourselves and the world we live in that celebrates the sacredness and sovereignty of the person, the sacredness of the earth, and the partnership between them.

Over the past couple of years, I have drawn on this perspective to write an ongoing series of essays called *David's Desk* which Lorian sends out to its mailing list once a month. This book is a collection of some of these essays in a new format to make them more available. While not exactly a formal introduction to Incarnational Spirituality, I hope they convey the attitude and spirit behind this approach. If they kindle your interest, you can investigate further by going to the Lorian website. In any event, I hope that these essays may at least be sparks to nourish and increase your own flame of incarnation.

David Spangler
June 2009

The Flame of Incarnation

Spirituality in Everyday Life

At a lecture recently, I was asked "What is the use of spirituality in everyday life? How can it help us address the problems of the world? We need action, not meditation."

This is not an unusual question. I imagine most, if not all, spiritual teachers are asked it from time to time. Nor is it an unfair question. We are a practical species, after all, and we want to know not only how things work but how they will work for us and what benefit we will derive. And while the question as stated perpetuates a common misunderstanding that spirituality is otherworldly (and that meditation is what spirituality is all about), it carries a genuine caring of the questioner for the wellbeing of others and the world.

It also expresses the perplexity of a person raised in an industrial, technological, strongly materialistic culture faced with problems such as climate change, nuclear proliferation, the widening of the economic and social disparity between rich and poor nations, and terrorism that are themselves the by-products of such a culture and which are resistant to purely industrial, technological, or materialistic solutions.

The times we are in create stress, and we naturally want to relieve that stress, preferably as soon as possible, which means a desire for quick fixes. Like a magical spell, the speed of technological processes has entranced us and turned us into impatient, short-term thinkers who want our solutions and gratifications now. Consider the irritation we may feel if our computers take thirty seconds to access a website instead of five. And when it comes to spirituality, if I can't learn it and do it after a weekend course, then what use is it?

But spirituality has never been about short-term experiences or solutions. It is part of the "long wave" of human experience and growth. It some ways it's not even about solutions but about the process of arriving at solutions, about how we think, how we feel, how we see, how we engage.

It is common to say that spirituality is about being rather than about doing. But this is a largely artificial and rhetorical distinction. When I act, I act from my being, and that I can act at all is because I have beingness. But we can also say that we come into being through our actions, that being itself is an action.

I think of incarnation as an ongoing act of will

in relationship and engagement with the world. So, spirituality is as much about doing as it is about being. Indeed, I would say that spirituality and spiritual practice are about uniting the apparent dichotomies of being and doing into a unity, a wholeness of active presence.

Imagine a group of people in a room engaging in a craft project. Some are knitting, some are crocheting, some are doing needlepoint, and some are sewing. Each of these is a separate and distinct art requiring specific skills; they are different ways of doing. But all of them require and use hand and eye coordination and the fine motor skills of finger work. If I am "all thumbs," it doesn't matter which craft I'm doing, the results will be mediocre at best. I may even fail completely. With practice, though, I can master the coordination and muscle movements necessary to skillfully manipulate the knitting needles or the crochet hook or the needle and thread. As I do, I can concentrate more and more on the pattern I'm trying to create—the sweater, the picture, the dress, the quilt—and less and less on just getting my fingers to do the right thing.

In this example, spirituality should be seen not as a technique, such as knitting or sewing, but as the skill of hand-eye coordination and the fine motor skills that make all these arts and crafts possible. In other words, spirituality is metaphorically the underlying skill that enables the doing of these crafts, not the crafts themselves. Spirituality is the equivalent of good coordination. It is the ability of my fingers to do the right thing in the moment. It is the "muscle knowing" of the appropriate action that honors the stitch or the knit I'm making, the larger pattern I'm working with, the spirit of the craft itself, and the joy I have in participating in this craft.

What does this mean in our everyday world? Well, think about those qualities or actions that we call "spiritual." What might they have in common? Think about love, compassion, caring, forgiveness, peacefulness, integrity, coherency. What do they do? Think of them in terms of "I/hand" coordination, that is, how I blend, connect, and engage with my world. Being loving or compassionate doesn't make me otherworldly. Rather it gives me the "fine motor skills" of human relationship that can enhance communication, cooperation, understanding, effectiveness. Any of the spiritual qualities enable me to "stitch" or "knit" the human fabric together more closely. And if I have cultivated an inner peace, I'm more able to focus on the larger patterns of humanity and the sacred, on the wholeness of things around me and the wholeness of the world, rather than focusing on the fumbling of my fingers as I try to master a particular technique.

It could be said we face so many planetary problems precisely because we have become "all thumbs" where the world, where nature, and where our fellow human beings are concerned. We are not coordinated. We are dropping stitches, losing threads, missing connections, and breaking patterns all over the place. We are fumbling through life.

Spiritual practice and techniques, from meditation and prayer to ritual and reflection, are our finger exercises to develop the skills of coordination. Love coordinates. Peacefulness coordinates. Compassion and forgiveness coordinate. They are the fine motor skills of good human relationships. Attunement to nature coordinates and is the fine motor skill of good environmental relationships.

The Flame of Incarnation

Yes, a person can get lost in just doing the finger exercises and never picking up a needle and thread. But simply trying to act—to sew more, knit more, crochet more—without being more coordinated is not going to solve the problem. It's only going to give us more of the tangle we already have.

Thresholds

I want to tell you about three phone calls I've had recently. The first was from a man I know slightly and whom I had not heard from for several years. It was a distressing call as he was facing total ruin in his life as a result of the current economic meltdown. He had just lost his job, was deeply in debt, and was facing losing his home. He was staring into a very scary, unknown future rising like a wall before him towards which he was hurtling, and he was filled with panic. He needed to talk to someone and reached out to me.

The second call was from a man I knew a little better but also whom I had not seen in several years. The last we had talked he had become ill but then I heard no more other than that he had moved with his family from the area. Now he was back, and he told me a harrowing story of his descent through a most dark time of extreme pain, illness, financial loss, and family crisis. His whole life had been turned upside down and inside out and in the process he had discovered resources of inner strength and calm. He had found an inner light and creativity he had not known he had possessed. He wasn't quite recovered but he could see his way back. Having lost almost everything, he was now discovering and building a whole new life that was more attuned and wonderful than what he had had before.

The third call was from a close friend who had also been going through a very difficult time. I had not heard from him for close to a year and didn't know the extent of his troubles. But he called not with a tale of woe but with a report that having been on the verge of bankruptcy, his business had suddenly taken off. In the midst of the growing recession, he was unexpectedly and suddenly prospering because his particular skills and services were valuable to businesses that were facing economic problems. And everything else in his life was alchemically coming together as well in a new alloy of joy and wholeness.

These three calls were from people facing, moving through, or emerging from a threshold of transformation. In this they seemed to me to represent the nature of the times in which we live. These are threshold times for all of us as humanity faces profound forces of change at work in the world today.

Interestingly, the threshold in all three calls was essentially the same. It was a threshold of dissolution and loss: loss of power, loss of livelihood, loss of home, loss of habitual ways of doing things, and in a deep way, loss of a familiar identity. The instinct when confronted with such losses is to hold on, to wrap around and cling to all that's familiar as one is hurtled forward. The

The Flame of Incarnation

river of one's life becomes frighteningly turbulent as it crashes against unexpected boulders and twists around unforeseen bends, and we grip all the more tenaciously and rigidly to the form of the boat we've been riding. But like a birth canal, often the channel of transformation towards which we are racing is navigated most skillfully if we can relax and let go and let the momentum carry us through. Floundering and striking out or fighting back with denial and anger only increases the likelihood of bashing against the boulders.

Not all thresholds are transformative in this way or have to be navigated through loss and pain, but I think given the tenor of the times, we will be seeing more and more of these kinds of experiences. Humanity has accumulated a lot of baggage that it will have to give up to win through to a more humane and blessing-full future, not least of which is its sense of identity as something special for whom the planet is a plaything and piggy bank to do with as it wishes. The current economic downturn is only a shadow of what may happen as we run up against climate change and finite limits to natural resources. This morning the news was full of speculation on the possible crippling impact on the already battered world economy if a full pandemic of the swine flu virus erupts, never mind the potential loss of millions of lives.

I am by instinct an optimist, and my inner experiences are unfailing in giving me faith in humanity's innate goodness and spiritual capacities. At the same time, incarnation is the soul's version of an extreme sporting event, one filled with thrills and chills as we measure ourselves against the challenges of evolution and the rush of unfolding new potentials. My oldest son likes to hurl himself off the sides of mountains wearing only a thin set of paragliding wings, and I have friends that like to put themselves in small boats hurtling down river rapids. They deliberately bring themselves to thresholds of challenge because of the expanded sense of self that emerges on the other side. Souls do the same thing with life itself, I'm convinced!

So in addition to my optimism about the future, I think we are at one of those places in planetary and human life where the ride is about to get very fast and very interesting indeed.

If this is so, what can we do?

The first step is not to fear the thresholds. This is easier said than done of course, especially when the threshold threatens to take everything from us that we think of as ourselves, maybe even our physical life, and also when it comes upon us unexpectedly, as such thresholds can do. But fear is additional baggage we don't need to carry while navigating the rapids of change. The anchor of denial and resistance only makes us less maneuverable, not more.

In talking to the gentleman of the first call, there was little I could do for him in a practical way; he lives thousands of miles away. My first task was to listen as he poured out his fear, anger and despair. And just telling him not to be afraid, I knew, wouldn't be very helpful as from his perspective he had every reason to be afraid. His fear was a center around which he was coalescing himself; that is, in a paradoxical way, it gave him a sense of stability, albeit a painful one.

A trained counselor might have been able to help him a good deal more than I could, for my perceptions are not psychological but energetic. So I couldn't give him mental or emotional techniques to help him deal with his fear. But I could ask him to take some time to honor himself and his fear and to deliberately grieve over what he was losing. Part of his familiar life *was* dying, and to deny it was to lose touch with the transformative energies at work in his life. Taking time to deliberately stop and listen to his fears would, I knew, give the turbulence of his energy field a chance to steady itself and be held by his own attentiveness. Just flailing about mentally and emotionally with a fearful energy doesn't go anywhere, but focusing on the fear and making it speak coherently and calmly to oneself helps to shift one's inner experience from feeling helpless to feeling a sense of power, at least the power to listen, which is a start.

As he began to listen and to calm, he began to list positive things he could do, and each time he came up with a fearful objection to doing those things, I asked him to go back and honor the energy of the suggestion he had made. It might not work out but taking a positive step in a helpful direction was better energetically than doing nothing.

What I felt was my most important suggestion was that while looking for new employment he also seek out some form of volunteer work he could do to help others in a similar position as himself. If we can find an inner generosity to help others, it keeps our own creative energy from collapsing and constricting around the hard knot of our personal fears. Such constriction only makes our own process of manifestation much more difficult energetically.

Had his phone call been the last one, I could have told him the stories of the others. Part of his challenge was that he was at the start of the process, just facing the threshold and unsure of himself and his future. But the other two men had gone through experiences at least as bad and in one case much worse than what he was facing, and they had come out the other side feeling more powerful than before. They were different; they had been reborn. And they showed that a threshold is not the end. It's a passage, not a destination.

In our times, that may be the most important knowledge of all.

Surviving in Hard Times

Once I had a rich aunt. Her husband had been very successful in business and upon his death had left her very well off. She was the oldest of my mother's many sisters and was a loving and gracious woman. I always loved visiting her. But for a wealthy woman, she had habits that were surprising to me. She was a generous woman, but she had a sense of scarcity as well. When we would go out to dinner, for instance, she would take all the sugar packets from the table and put them into her purse before we left. I asked her about this once, and she said that since the restaurant had given them to her by putting them on the table, she was going to take them. "You never know when you might need sugar,"

she said to me even though she bought sugar regularly from the grocery store.

She did the same with packets of ketchup and mustard and other condiments. I wondered about how she could be so wealthy and so giving a person yet at the same time scrounge all kinds of little things that stores and restaurants put out for people to use. My mother explained it was because she had gone through the Great Depression as a teenager and had suffered the extremes of hardship that their family had gone through. If something were free or there for the taking, she would take it like a squirrel taking nuts to store for the winter.

Mom had lived through that time, too, but she had been much younger and had been less impacted. Her oldest sister, though, had come out of the Depression filled with a fear of poverty and a survivor's need to take care of herself. That she became such a giving woman in later years was a testimony to the overall largeness of her character, but through the years I recognized that a fear had settled in her from that time and was still present decades and many full bank accounts later.

Now we are on the brink of hard times again. For many people, even being on that brink seems preferable to the possibility we'll tumble over it, as they experience their finances and savings beginning to drop in free fall. We are in the worst financial crisis since the 1930's, perhaps moving into another Depression, a frightening thought for a Baby Boomer generation that on the whole has always known relative abundance and few persistent, threatening crises. Soon we may all be scrounging sugar packets!

The situation is made worse by the atmosphere

of fear in our society, which is chronic. Fear is often cultivated as a tactic in commerce, government and, I'm sorry to say, spirituality. Fear is dramatic and motivational. Fear sells as much as sex does. Fear can be a source of power. No wonder it's attractive to people and organizations with manipulation on their minds. With so much fear in the collective energy field, it's hard to avoid it or be untouched by it. Fear makes hard times that much harder.

I wish I had financial advice to offer you that would save you any and all losses, but that's not my forte, unfortunately. However, I do have some thoughts about surviving hard times from an energy stand point. Here's my Twelve-Point Plan!

Open and Flowing

It's a fact of physiology that when we're angry or fearful, blood flow in the brain becomes constricted and shifts from the frontal lobes where creative thought takes place to the older brain centers that govern fight or flight. In an emergency situation, this may be useful to take swift instinctive action, but when this happens, we're in effect giving ourselves a lobotomy. Many of the situations we face today don't require immediate fight or flight but sustained creative thought. This is certainly true of getting through a financial crisis. We want to be relaxed enough for blood flow to reach the brain centers that really need it.

The same is true for our energy field. Healthy energy is energy that is open and flowing. When we are fearful, our energy constricts, we tighten up, and connections with the larger world—and the spiritual worlds—diminish or shut down. We lose touch with expanded resources of spirit, creativity, and energy right when we need them. To survive and prosper in hard times—indeed, at any time—we need our energy open, clean, clear, and flowing

How you do this is ultimately unique to your situation and to your innate capacities and character. But here are twelve simple suggestions to help with this process

1. Physical Activity

Nothing gets your energy flowing like physical activity. It can be as simple as breathing. How often have you been told when you're feeling panicky to just take some deep breaths? One way is to breathe rhythmically. Breath down into your feet and from there into the earth. Breath up into your head and from there into the heavens. Breath out into your arms and from there into the life of nature and the world. Breath energy into your connections and your wholeness, and breath that wholeness back into your heart and mind. Walking is another wonderful and easy way to restore energy flow. Do something that gets your heart pumping, your blood flowing, and your body throwing off the chemical toxins that fear can produce.

2. Making Fear Your Friend

I'm someone who dislikes cold weather. I can just feel myself tightening up. Part of it is my lungs which are weak from chronic asthma since childhood; cold air makes my lungs hurt and makes it harder for me to breathe. But my wife Julie, who grew up in a colder climate than I did, always tells me, "Make the cold your friend," and when I do, when I reach out and acknowledge it and try not to resist it, in fact my body does relax and I do feel warmer.

My wife was in our bank recently and happened to see our bank manager. "Tough times," he said. "Yes," Julie replied, "but remember, all we need to fear is fear itself." He laughed and replied, "True, but fear is scary!"

Fear *is* scary. It's like the cold. It makes us want to tighten up and preserve what we have, even if we lose the openness and flow of our energy in the process. It makes us want to avoid it and run away from what is frightening us. But the best thing to do energetically is to face it and acknowledge the fearful energy itself. This takes courage but just facing the fear can empower us.

And sometimes fear is justified. Fear, like pain, can tell us something is amiss and needs our attention. It can call us to action to correct a situation. Or it can be a fear of the unknown, of what we can't name or foresee. The changes might be good and leave us stronger than before, but in the moment we don't know that and can't be sure. So there's fear.

Listening deeply to your fears can defuse their charge and lead you to make important changes in your life. In this listening, though, you want to recognize that the *energy* or *feeling* of a fear is not necessarily equivalent to the situation that's producing it, anymore than the shadow a person casts is necessarily an accurate measurement of his body size. Minor things can cause us to panic, especially if others are sharing that fear and magnifying it. I want to listen to the *content* of the fear—the actual facts of the situation and their potential consequences—and not just to the emotional and imaginal drama and energy it may project. And if it's fear of the unknown, I want to pay attention to the possibilities and the positive outcomes as well as the potentially negative ones.

3. No Blame

When times are tough and fear runs rampant through our collective energy, it's easy to look for people to blame for the problems. It's important to identify wrong actions and structures, to see what's broken, and to find responsible and appropriate ways of fixing it. Where there is responsibility, there should be consequences. But playing the blame game is always energetically poisonous. Blame comes from fear and anger, emotions that either constrict or make our energy field turbulent and hurtful; blame is an attack upon another, expressing an implicit—and sometimes an explicit—desire to punish. It keeps our own energy field inflamed, which works against openness, flow, and connectedness. Resist the temptation to find victims and to assign blame, even while you determine responsibility. You want to fix and heal things, not destroy people. Taking time to blame people and vent your anger may feel good in the moment, like a sugar high, but it can lead to a diabetes of the soul resulting in blindness and the amputation of the spiritual limbs through which we can love and hold another. We all do stupid things. We all make mistakes. We all have greed and lust somewhere in our soul's history. And we have all been forgiven. Practicing forgiveness is the insulin that counteracts the ravages of blame.

4. Not Everything Is Falling Apart: Keeping Perspective

When your 401(k) retirement account is vanishing before your eyes, it's not at all surprising to feel that everything is falling apart. But it's not, at least not unless an asteroid is about to hit the earth and wipe out all life. Only some things are falling apart! Others are most likely holding together quite nicely or even improving. Fear focuses your attention down onto what is frightening you, causing you to lose a larger, more holistic awareness. No wonder your energy tightens up. You need to broaden your vision again and restore perspective. Yes, some things are going wrong, and you want to give them an honest appraisal and take appropriate action. But what is going right? Take time to look around and see. Don't let your fear collapse your world into a small bubble of disaster. Reclaim your citizenship as part of a larger world in which things *do* work and are working well.

The challenge is to avoid falling into drama. Some drama is fun; we all enjoy a good story. But drama for its own sake simply keeps our energy turbulent, not flowing. Life reads our needs in the clear pool of our being, but it can't do so if the surface is constantly churning.

5. Positive Thoughts

In times of fear and panic we are told to think positively and that our greater good and our ability to manifest depend on holding only positive thoughts and feelings. This can create a curious backlash of anger and fear towards ourselves when negative thoughts and feelings creep in, as they are bound to do if only by leakage from the collective. This double reaction of having a negative thought and then feeling negatively about ourselves because of that can definitely constrict our energy.

Positive thinking is not a club to hold over our heads. It might be better characterized as relaxed and open thinking, the kind of thinking and feeling that enables us to stay connected, expansive, and flowing. Paying attention to what's right in our life and in our world, for instance, can restore a sense of balance and positivity. Often thinking of joyous memories, experiences, thoughts, and the like can shift our mood. As Dr. William Bloom—one of the best teachers in managing your energy fields that I know—points out in his book, *The Endorphin Effect*, they can trigger a flood of the brain's "happy chemicals," the endorphins that can have immediate and positive effects upon our body chemistry. And a happy body is one that generates an energy field that is more clear and flowing.

While holding positive thoughts and emotions is advantageous, positive thinking itself is not "Hallmark Card thinking." It's really an ongoing awareness that all truly *is* well with the world, with life, and with oneself. It's also a commitment not to mindlessly pass on fears but to bring positive energy, images, ideas, and feelings into the lives of others, to help them attune to the wellness at the heart of the world. If fear is the Balrog of our time, then positive thinking is like Gandalf standing courageously on the bridge saying, "You shall not pass!"

6. Connections

When our energies constrict, we can become isolated. The laws of manifestation and blessing operate in a condition of wholeness and connectedness. If we cut ourselves off because we're fearful, we limit our communication and contact with the larger world from which help may come. And we may lose our capacity to give help, to be there for others. To restore our energy connections, we want to mindfully and appropriately reach out to others and to nature. The simplest step is to talk out our fears with another, not in a needy way—and certainly not just to pass them on and make another afraid—but as calmly and openly as we can, and then to listen quietly and openly if another shares their fears with us.

Discovering how you can help another and what links of community and shared resources may exist around you is a vital way to open your energy and get it flowing again. Abundance flows through wholeness and connectedness; it's not a private miracle delivered to us in our isolation and neediness. You want your energy to expand out and to participate in the wellbeing of the world, for then the world can find you to give you its gifts of blessing which are always there for you.

7. Generosity

When times are tough, the tough get giving. Whether with our time, our energy, or our money, being generous is one of the fastest and surest ways to open our hearts and minds and restore a flow. But here's a secret: giving is, well, a *gift*. It's not a transaction. The nature of generosity is that it's a true giving of oneself with no expectation or desire of a return. If we expect something in return, that expectation can itself become a tightening and constricting force within our energy field, especially if it turns into disappointment, anger, or frustration that our generosity wasn't reciprocated or properly appreciated, at least not in a way we recognized or anticipated. A gift frees both the giver and the receiver; it doesn't bind them together in chains of obligation and expectation.

8. Gratefulness

The nature of a financial crisis is to focus on scarcity, on what we lack or are losing. Fear, anger, and frustration arise as a consequence. To shift this dynamic, we want to focus on what we have and to be grateful for it. More than just a catchy song lyric, "counting our blessings" is good energy hygiene, as long as it opens our hearts to gratefulness. Gratitude is not an attitude of dependency but a recognition of interdependency and the ways in which so much of what we have and enjoy—even our very lives—comes from someone or something else. Gratefulness is not simply appreciation, though it certainly is that; it's an awareness of the interconnectedness of life and of our membership in a vast community of being. That awareness opens our hearts and restores our sense of participation and flow. Saying "Thank you" to life, to the Sacred, and particularly to our fellow human beings becomes a blessing to all concerned and lifts us above the images of scarcity and loss that otherwise seek to bring us down.

9. Appreciating the Times

It may seem hard to extend our gratefulness and appreciation to the time in which we live and the challenges it presents—to financial crisis, global climate change, terrorism, wars, energy depletion, and any other disasters looming on the horizon. It would be much easier to appreciate an era of good feeling, peace and calm stability! But difficult times are also times of growth, of new insights and opportunities, of creativity, and of emergence. If I can't fight the program, I might as well go with it! Resisting the flow of the times is futile; we live in this moment of history facing these challenges. The future will unfold based on our decisions and action. Of course this is scary! But if we retreat, our energy will constrict, our creative input will be lost, and the future will come anyway, and even more likely in a form we don't like. The times *are* challenging but they are also creative and open to new birth, new potentials, and new possibilities. Aligning with that side of things definitely gets our energy flowing and opening again.

10. Stand in Sovereignty

In my work which I call Incarnational Spirituality, sovereignty is the wholeness between soul and personality that enables us to be self-governing, giving us the power to make choices, to express intentionality, and to unfold our individual identity. It is the source of those unique gifts that only we can contribute to life. To "stand in sovereignty" is to attune to this inner wholeness and to honor our identity—to honor ourselves—and the connections we form with life. Our holistic nature as spiritual beings is always more expansive and powerful than the circumstances that beset us. When we claim that expansiveness, we truly open our hearts and minds to a larger dimension of self, and our energy heightens and rises to meet this occasion. How can we meet the challenges of hard times, or of any times, if we undermine, dishonor, or diminish ourselves and our sense of identity? How can we be creative if we doubt our ability to be generative? Where will fear stop if we allow our identities, our thoughts and feelings, to be shaped by the fears of others, particularly those who may benefit from our being afraid? Big challenges call for big people, and the bigness of spirit and life within each of us is larger than most of us suspect. Standing in our sovereignty opens the doors to spaciousness within us and to an empowered relationship with life around us.

11. Be Loving

The previous ten suggestions can all be summed up in two words: be loving. Love really is the answer to human problems: love of oneself, love of others, love of where one is, love of what one is doing, love of nature, love of life, love of the world, love of spirit in all its wonder and splendor. Love sets our energy free. It opens us and puts us in a flow with spirit and life on many levels. Love is the true secret behind manifestation. It wears many faces—caring, compassion, awareness, courage, creativity—but whichever face it shows in the moment, it is always our most powerful response to hard and challenging times.

Love is magical. As Shakespeare said, the more we give of it, the more we have. It operates in a gifting economy, one that can only know abundance. At a time when the world tells us to be afraid and that we're losing everything, love tells us we are safe and we are generative sources of wealth for ourselves and for others. Love is the power behind the miracles of loaves and fishes, the power that opens purses, wallets, cupboards, refrigerators, pantries, and most of all, hearts, to allow a flow of sharing that reminds us that we *can* take care of each other. Where there is love, we *can* help each other. Where there is love, there is a will to overcome separateness and the fear separateness can bring. We can be a strength of heart, mind and will for each other. These may be hard times, but with love, we are not hard people.

12. Be "God-full"

I have put this last for emphasis, but it could just as easily be the first step. God is vital. God is also a mystery. In my language it is the Generative Mystery. Throughout history people have called this ultimate or foundational reality many things and have seen it in many ways. But what we call it or how we see it is less important than understanding what its presence is within us. It truly makes us home in the universe. If we are open and flowing, it is because this ultimate presence is open and flowing. When we love, our love is magnified hundreds, thousands, millions of times because this ultimate presence is loving.

The Findhorn Foundation community was founded

on a very simple premise: put God first in your life and everything you need comes to you. The Founders of Findhorn proved this time and again in their lives, and Findhorn itself grew and prospered as a result of this simple principle of manifestation.

For me, putting God first means to be "God-full," full of the qualities of this generative, loving presence as much as I, as a finite individual, can be. Before I see the world, let my eyes be full of God. Before I open my heart, let my heart be full of God. Before I think, let my mind be full of God. Before I speak, let my mouth be full of God. Before I act, let my limbs be full of God. Let my personal world be God's world first, a God-full world, and I know everything else is added.

Godfulness is simply recognizing the primacy of a presence of love, spaciousness, grace, generativity, caring, and creativity in the world and in myself. How can a mere financial crisis compare to that? The Generative Mystery cannot go bankrupt. It is not subject to scarcity. We never run out of God.

The Real Question

Sometimes it seems obligatory for a spiritual teacher to have a collection of numbered steps for doing various things: ten steps for this, twelve steps for that, seven steps to do this other thing, and so on. I've never quite achieved that; my sense of spirit has been more like a ramp than a series of steps, a continuum along which we move instead of a ladder we climb.

But difficult times create new possibilities, and even old dogs can learn new tricks. So here are my Twelve Steps for Surviving Hard Times.

Will they work? Will our lives be better if we practice them?

The real question is what will happen to ourselves and our world if we don't.

Living The Times

Recently I took part in a small conference that had the encouraging title "You Were Born for Such a Time as This!" The theme of this event was focused on the potentials for creative living and success that each of us have within us. Sitting on a panel waiting my turn to speak, my thoughts went in a different direction, though. What, I thought, was meant by "such a time as this?"

Clearly the conference organizers had a couple of things in mind. One was the economic crisis facing the United States and the world at large. Another was the general sense of transformation abroad in the land as old habits and ways of doing things confronted a rapidly changing world that demanded new approaches and solutions. But not everyone was experiencing "this time" in exactly that way.

For instance, my youngest son works in a store

Living the Times

located in a local shopping mall. When I went to visit him one day recently, I discovered the mall was filled with shoppers for whom no economic recession seemed to be happening at all. The happy faces of people moving in and out of the shops purchasing things bore no relationship to the news of job layoffs, unemployment, and stores going bankrupt that I had just seen on the evening news before coming to the shopping center.

So what was "such a time as this?" For the people in that mall, it did not appear to be one of economic hardship. That got me thinking about time not as past, present and future but as the unique condition that each of us inhabits. For instance, as I go outside after a long winter and glory in the sunshine and spring flowers, a friend of mine in Australia is putting on warmer clothes and preparing for the growing cold of winter. His time, his season, is not the same as mine.

I had taken my place at the panel not knowing what I was going to say. But when my turn came, I knew I would begin by saying, "We do not live in one time. We live in four of them." The subject of this essay then flowed from that thought.

We inhabit four times. The first of these is World Time. This is the time we all commonly share by virtue of being on earth at the beginning of the twenty-first century. This is the time the conference organizers had in mind when they came up with the phrase, "You were born for such a time as this!" This is the time as portrayed by national news broadcasts and other media; it is the collective history we are all living. This time is one of global climate change, threats to the ecology, economic recession and meltdown, wars and terrorism, and the possibilities of pandemics. It is also a time of space flights, globalization, cures for ancient diseases, and the development of a planetary mind electronically mediated through the Internet and planetary communication technology. It is a time when the challenges and the opportunities are world-size and humanity is truly experiencing itself as a planetary species.

World time is what humanity as a whole experiences, and the challenge is with its scale. Over and over again, I hear people asking me, "How can I make a difference? The problems are so vast and I am just one person. What can I do?" And the answer individually, at least at a physical level, would appear to be, "not much." There is very little that my actions by themselves, however enlightened, will do to stop the loss of the arctic ice, restore millions of lost jobs, or halt terrorism around the world. Even the President of the United States, arguably the most powerful individual on earth, cannot by himself accomplish these things.

To inhabit world time is to feel overwhelmed and possibly disempowered for the world is so large and we are so small. If it is the only time to which we pay attention, we can risk going a little crazy. Everything can seem so out of control, rushing towards one catastrophe or another carrying us along with it.

And we cannot avoid it. We are part of the world, and world time impacts us in various ways irresistibly, unstoppably, and impersonally.

By contrast, the second time that we live in is very personal. It is your time and my time. It is Individual Time. It is what we are experiencing—the challenges and opportunities we are facing—in our own personal lives.

When my youngest daughter was born, my wife's

sister was with us to help. In advanced stages of liver cancer, she had only a couple of months yet to live. I will never forget Merrily holding Maryn, each in their own very different individual time, a life going out cradling a life coming in, love flowing between them both.

In any given neighborhood, there are those being born, those who are dying, those who are getting their first job, those who are retiring from their last one; there are some who are losing everything and others finding abundance; there are those experiencing despair and those knowing hope and promise.

Personal time takes the events of world time and translates them into the unique contours of our individuality. The result may move in directions very different from the world at large. Prosperity may be everywhere yet I may be facing bankruptcy; economies are failing, yet I may be generating wealth.

The key is that, unlike world time, individual time is lived at a human scale. I may not feel I can influence the world but I can definitely influence my own life. My decisions, my intentionality, my actions—or my lack of the same—can immediately and profoundly change what happens in the sphere of personal time. Although events can seem overwhelming in my life, I still know that potentially I can make a difference. I possess the ability to choose and to act. World time can seem to be the product of vast, impersonal forces but individual time is hand-made, so to speak.

Personal time is the time we are most concerned with. Events in the world at large may trouble or inspire us, but it's the challenge of our jobs, of meeting the mortgage, of keeping healthy, of raising a family, and of putting food on the table that will consume most of our attention.

The Flame of Incarnation

This individual time is made up of ordinary tasks, most of them repeated in one way or another each day.

The third time we inhabit is less obvious than either of the other two. Personal, individual time is in our face daily and world time is all about us in the news of events transpiring on our globe. But there is a Deep Time or a New Time that is within us and within the world, and it is where the power of transformation lies.

This might be called "spiritual time" for it exists in the depths of our spirit. It is the ability to stand in and experience not an "eternal now" but an eternal new. It is renewal time, the inner state in which all things are beginning and new directions can be both envisioned and chosen in spite of our history. It is the time of transformation. It is the promise embodied in the phrase, "Behold, I make all things new."

This time is like a stillness within us. It's where the rushing momentum of world time and personal time comes to a halt, where world time and personal time step back and make room for new possibilities to emerge. It is a place of vision, a place of hope, a place of power.

For a good part of my life, I was involved with the New Age movement. The vision of a New Age is still a strong and powerful one for me, and while the movement itself may have lost credibility and the term one of derision, the idea that we can create a new time, a new history, a new world for humanity is the most powerful and necessary idea that we have. How else to meet the challenges of our age except with an acknowledgement of our ability to change, to move in fresh directions, and to embody new visions? To think otherwise is to abandon hope and give in to despair.

The challenge with the New Age was that it was

seen as an event in world time, usually an apocalypse of some sort leading to a new world. But the New Age is an expression of deep time or new time. It is a recognition and affirmation that within us is a place, a consciousness, where we can think anew, see anew, and act anew. It is affirmation that transformation is possible. It is a call to inhabit and live from the creativity of deep time, new time.

This is a profoundly spiritual place for it taps our most fundamental creative spirit and imagination. It is the place where we can say, "Whatever our yesterdays have been like, our tomorrows can be different." We can reach this place in a variety of ways: inspiration, art, prayer, meditation, service, reflection. All it requires is that we accept the possibility that we can stop, take a breath, look again, see in new ways, change our minds, open our hearts to potential, and have the courage to step forth in new directions.

Both world time and personal time need the renewal that deep, new time can bring. Old ways of being are not working and are making the global situation worse. We need to become new

But even inhabiting this powerful inner time is not the wholeness of our power nor the full answer to the challenges of world or personal time. For that we need the fourth time. We need Our Time.

Our time is simply the time we co-create together, and if we do so out of the vision and inspiration, the spirit and energy of New Time, this can be very powerful indeed. As I said earlier, no one person can change the world, however enlightened, however noble, however well-positioned and influential he or she may be. To alter world time is beyond the capability of anyone. But it is not beyond the capability of all of us. It is not beyond the power of individuals working in partnership and collaboration. It is not beyond the power of our time.

At the heart of world time is the momentum of history. At the heart of personal time is the mystery and wonder of individuality. At the heart of deep, new time is the creative spirit. But at the heart of our time is love.

If there is any force that can bring together the four times in a convergence of heart, mind, will, and transformation, it's love. Love is what brings us and binds us together. Love can be as simple as respecting each other. It can be as complex and powerful as dedicating our lives in affection, trust, and mutuality to each other. But whatever form it takes, it draws us together, opens our hearts and minds to each other, and releases the power that only collaboration can bring. In our time the other times find their fulfillment and their promise. In our time we can make a difference that is not available or possible to us in either world time or personal time and which is only a potential in new time.

There is a power that lies in living in the now as many teachers and philosophies proclaim. But the power that we need comes from living in time, in the four times through which the world, the self, the spirit, and the community are brought together in creative potential and transformative partnership.

Indeed, these are the times for which we were born.

Spiritual Energy

A friend of mine wrote to me recently and commented that we needed to "bring spiritual energies into the world situation." I heartily agreed. But later I got to thinking, just what was I agreeing to?

What are spiritual energies?

This is one of those concepts that we use and assume that everyone knows what we mean. And I think on the whole we do have an intuition about what spiritual energies are. We may well agree that whatever else they are, spiritual energies are good and helpful and thus to be desired. On the other hand, what you mean by this phrase and what I mean by it may not be the same. To one person, bringing spiritual energies into the world may mean converting people to a particular faith or belief, while to another it may mean something more intangible and subtle, a kind of vibrational uplift.

I don't intend to produce a definition of spiritual

Spiritual Energy

energies that will satisfy all people under all circumstances. Mrs. Spangler didn't raise her little ol' boy child to be that presumptuous—or stupid! But I would like to share my own thought process as I considered just what this concept means to me; perhaps you will find it helpful and stimulating to your own thinking.

One way to think about spiritual energies is to put them into a category like "Washington apples," "Idaho potatoes," or "French wines." This is to say, they are energies that come from a particular locality or source. If they come from "spirit," they are "spiritual energies." If they come from the world, they are, well, "world energies." OK, that makes sense. It's certainly a simple and satisfying way to look at it. Until, that is, I begin to ask, "What is spirit?"

My mother and father are both in the non-physical realms, having died some years ago. If I receive energy from them, is that spiritual energy? They are, after all, spirits in a sense. What about energy from an invisible nature spirit. Is that spiritual energy? Or how about a blessing from an angel, or even (let's go all out) an archangel? Surely that must be spiritual energy! But then, what about energy from the Sacred?

In other words, what part of the non-physical realms is the source of "spiritual energy"? All of it? Some of it? Some levels but not other levels? What makes one layer of being capable of expressing spiritual energy and not another layer?

Thus there are problems when I define spiritual energy by source. For one thing, we use the word "spiritual" in two distinct ways that are often confused. It can mean "holy," "uplifting," and "life-affirming," or it can mean "not physical" or "not material." For

The Flame of Incarnation

many people, if it isn't made up of matter or doesn't have a body, it's a spirit and thus spiritual. But just as all French wines are not alike in quality or taste, and some Washington apples are good for cooking but not necessarily for eating raw, not all non-physical manifestations or energies are uplifting or life-affirming. Is a haunting spiritual?

A Granny apple has a different taste from a Pippin, a Macintosh or a Honeycrisp. A merlot is different from a champagne. Given all the different kinds of energies we might experience, what "flavor" is a spiritual energy? How do we distinguish it, if not by its source? Here is where the effect of an energy, what it does to us, for us, or within us, is important.

So far, I've been focusing on the word "spiritual," but the word "energy" is also equally undefined in this context. What, after all, is a spiritual energy? What is energy anyway?

In physics, energy has a very clear definition. It's a measure of the capacity to do work. Or put another way, it's a measure of the capacity to promote or produce an effect. Energy makes things happen.

What work does spiritual energy measure? What does it make happen?

Here I am helped in my deliberations by a quick trip to my dictionary. It tells me that the word spirit comes from a Latin root meaning "to breath." Spirit is the power to breath, or in a broader sense, the power to animate and to give life. It is the energy of life. Spirit makes life happen. Life is the effect of spirit. And life here means more than just biological existence. It means the whole measure of possibility, wholeness, relationship, emergence, creativity, and potential that any organism

Spiritual Energy

may possess—and humans more than most. To breathe is to provide the energy that makes thought possible, feeling possible, love possible, creativity possible, whole cultures and civilizations possible.

This puts me in mind of something Jesus said in the gospel of John, "I come that they may have life and have it abundantly." This seems to me an excellent example of what spiritual energies do: they promote and foster life and do so abundantly on all levels and in all ways that life may manifest.

This means several things to me. First, it means that spiritual energies make possible the expression and use of other kinds of energies, energies of the mind or the heart, of the body or of the soul. For all these other energies proceed from and express life. Second, spiritual energies quicken and enhance the capacities of life, not only to grow but to be whole and coherent, to connect, to relate, and to engage. Life is an integrated open system that produces energy and gives of itself. Spiritual energies enhance this capacity to be open and giving, to be alive.

Third, it means that spiritual energies refer to a function rather than to a source. The effect of spiritual energies is independent of the source of those energies. Water is necessary for life, but it doesn't matter whether the water comes from a lake, a river, a well, or a rain barrel. (Of course, the source of the water can affect its purity and its taste, but that's another matter…and a matter of taste!)

This means that spiritual energies don't have to come from, well, "spirit." They are not the sole province of the non-physical, transpersonal, transcendent realms. They can come from us. We as physical, incarnate, personal individuals can be generative sources of spiritual energy.

Fourth, spiritual energies don't have to look "religious" or transcendent. If the effect is to nourish life, to promote the conditions that help life prosper, and to empower someone to "have life abundantly," it is a spiritual energy. This could take the form of a smile, a hug, an act of courtesy, a moment of listening that helps another move through a stuck energy, a gift of kindness. The spiritual energy doesn't have to be "big," the kind that moves mountains and transforms whole nations. Helping a single heart or mind to be more open to the possibilities of life changes a world. We do ourselves and the universe a disservice when we think that spiritual energies must be spectacular, extraordinary, or dramatic.

Fifth, spiritual energies can and often do transcend limits, enabling us to go beyond boundaries, but they don't have to. I don't have to have unconditional love to express the spiritual energy—the life-affirming, heightening, quickening power—of love. If I can love only one person, and even that perhaps imperfectly and with limits, but my love still enhances the life of the other, am I not expressing a spiritual energy? I say this because I have seen people beat themselves up emotionally and mentally for "not being spiritual enough," when in fact within the limits of their capacities in the moment, they are acting in loving and empowering ways. After all, my well may not be very deep and the water from it not as pure and tasty as some, but it can still sustain life, and I can still give it freely.

Liberating the idea of spiritual energies from a purely transcendental or transpersonal context—and

Spiritual Energy

from the expectation they need to be extraordinary—is part of the teaching of incarnational spirituality. It let's me understand "spiritual energies" in a broader, accessible context. Then when someone says, "We need to bring more spiritual energies to the earth," I don't need to feel I have to be a spiritual Olympian to do so or depend on non-physical beings to do the work. The flow of spiritual energy into the world may begin with me, right now, just as I am, in the welcoming smile I give a stranger or the helping hand I offer a neighbor.

Decisions

In a letter to Jean Baptiste Le Roy in 1789, Benjamin Franklin wrote, "But in this world nothing can be said to be certain, except death and taxes." To this I would add a third certainty: decisions.

Everyday we make decisions, beginning with "Shall I get out of bed today?" Some are trivial, some are not; some have little effect, others can change our lives. Some decisions we can avoid, delay, and ignore; others we can't. They come upon us with all the unavoidability of a train speeding towards us down a track on which we are tied like the heroine in a melodrama. Even when we can avoid a decision that in itself is a decision.

Like it or not, we are all, like former President Bush, Deciders.

This fact has an interesting consequence on our

Decisions

relationship with the spiritual worlds. It has for millennia shaped and influenced our perception of this relationship and perhaps even the nature of those inner worlds themselves.

How we make decisions can be as important as the decisions themselves. Making a decision is a process of exercising the muscles of our individuality and sovereignty, and some techniques give greater inner fitness and core spiritual strength than others. Techniques can range from various forms of reasoning through intuition to simply flipping a coin. But down the centuries, one popular way can be summed up in one word: "guidance."

Decisions are risky because they carry consequences. All decisions are variations on the algorithm "If…then." If I do this, then this will happen. In effect, all decisions are ultimately choices between consequences, though it may not seem so in the moment. Deciding between an apple and a double chocolate tort is a choice not simply between desserts but between losing or gaining a pound or two.

Naturally, faced with consequences, we want the best outcomes possible, and for that we want the best information we can get with which to make our decision. Ideally we want information that will enable us to gain the outcome that carries the most pleasure, happiness, safety, and power and is the least damaging or threatening. We don't want painful consequences if we can avoid them. But in this world at least, we can't always guarantee this. Information is often incomplete and the variables that can affect an outcome are complex.

In such a situation, it's natural that we look for sources of information and help in the decision-making process that would seem to have a greater perspective than we do and that can, if not absolutely guarantee good consequences, at least tip the balance in favor of outcomes we will like. We look for help. We look for guidance. 49

My friend and Lorian colleague, Dorothy Maclean, recently returned from a lecture tour in Greece where she was taken to see the ancient site of the Oracle at Delphi. Delphi is a good symbol for a perception of the spiritual worlds and of non-physical beings as sources of help in our decision-making, even to the extreme of letting them become the Deciders in our stead. Consider for a moment how much of our thinking about the spiritual worlds and inner beings is wrapped up around the need and challenge of making decisions. When we think about "tuning in," meditating, or seeking inner help, are we usually thinking about what wisdoms and insights we can offer the spiritual realms from our human experience? Are we thinking of simply hanging out with inner friends in some imaginal Starbucks? No, chances are we are thinking about getting help, guidance, information, insights, and intuitions that will help us make decisions, or even being told what to do so the decisions are made for us by, presumably, wiser beings.

Working as a spiritual teacher over the years, I've seen people who are quite willing to surrender their power to me or to some other spiritual teacher or some inner source as a way of letting someone else—or something else—carry their burden of decision-making. I've seen individuals who, using some technique of attunement—whether pendulums or tarot cards, meditation or channeling—refer every decision of their lives to "guidance": what clothes to wear, what colors, what foods to eat, what books to read, even in the case of one woman when and whether to go to the bathroom, as if her bladder had no say in the matter. One wonders why people so addicted to guidance even bother to incarnate. A sponge would have more sovereignty and make more choices.

Most people, of course, don't go to such extremes. But by the same token, I've observed that when most people think of the inner worlds, they think of them in relationship to their decision-making. There is an assumption—backed up, as I said, by millennia of habit—that God, angels, inner teachers, animal spirits, the "dead," and various other non-physical beings are all there to give us guidance and help us make good decisions.

This has two major consequences. First, it distorts the nature of the inner worlds and greatly oversimplifies their complexity and diversity. Not all inner beings are able to or wish to offer guidance or advice, as many of them don't have a clue how human beings think and therefore how we make decisions. And even if they wish to give advice, it's not guarantee it will be good or useful. Their values and sense of consequences can be very different from ours. It's a bit like saying that a university exists solely to help me decide what job I should have and how I should do my work and that all the professors and staff are there only to perform that task (and that they can all perform it well). There are aspects of a university and people within it that can and will help me with my career but there are others that will not or cannot but which can offer me enrichment and empowerment in other ways.

The Flame of Incarnation

In addition, parts of the inner worlds adapt to this human desire for guidance and become "guidance-givers," whether or not this is a good thing. Where there is a need or a desire, something will respond; think of it as the opening of an ecological niche. There are life forms that will fill it. The niche of human need and decision-making definitely attracts those forms of inner life that are only too happy to offer advice, to substitute their sovereignty for ours, or to live parasitically through the choices they inspire. The only problem is that they don't suffer the consequences. We do.

The second consequence is that our own sovereignty and spiritual power are diminished. Making decisions is one way we develop our core spiritual strength. It is a sign of growing inner maturity and adulthood as much as learning to make our own choices is a sign of outer adulthood. Once we have learned how to make good decisions, to abdicate that capacity to any non-physical source (or for that matter to a physical one) lessens rather than enhances the possibilities that we will be able to create good consequences in our lives and the lives of others. It makes us vulnerable to inner "busybodies" who, like some human counselors I've known, exaggerate their own importance by giving guidance to others.

This does not mean that we can't get good—even very good—advice and direction from the spiritual worlds or that we shouldn't ask for help when we need it. There are times in all our lives when we are faced with decisions that seem to overwhelm us and when we need advice, information, perspectives, and insights beyond what we can find in ourselves. At such times, we can certainly reach beyond ourselves to others, both

Decisions

physical and non-physical, to be our allies in helping us make those decisions. The key is that we're not asking for guidance nor are we abdicating responsibility.

But that we have this right and power to seek help does not mean that this is the only—or even the main—relationship we can have with the non-physical dimensions of life. The inner worlds in my experience yearn for partnership and collaboration with us. They seek alliance. Many inner beings are in awe of the freedom and power represented by our capacity to make decisions and are empowered by it and learn from it. They seek us out not to tell us what to do but to observe how we transform information into wisdom and action through the power of choice. And paradoxically, I have found that it is by standing in my sovereignty and being willing to make my own decisions and accept responsibly the consequences of those decisions that I find myself in touch with those greater lives who truly can make decision-making an act of sacred partnership and help me create consequences that are better than I could have done on my own.

The Flame of Incarnation

No Muggles Here!

I don't know if your family is a fan of Harry Potter. Mine is. As the books have come out over the years, we have enjoyed more and more J. K. Rowling's engaging tale of the boy wizard and his friends. In fact, my youngest daughter and I have made a ritual of attending the midnight release parties at our local bookstore whenever a new Potter book has come out. When our four kids were younger, we would all gather in the living room and listen while my wife read the latest installment. It was fun and exciting. Rowling tells a great yarn.

In Harry Potter's universe, the world is divided into magic-users, known collectively as wizards and witches, and non-magic-users, known as muggles. Much of the fun of the books comes from reading the author's invention of new words and terms; as neologisms go, muggles is about as good as it gets. The big difference between Rowling's fictional universe and ours is that, however fun a word it is, there are no muggles here. We are all magic-users.

Now I'm not talking about fantasy magic, the kind that Harry uses or a wizard in a game of Dungeons and Dragons. Stories, while fun, deceive us about magic by turning it into something implausible. We come to think of magic as wizards hurling thunderbolts and flying through the air.

But there is an everyday magic that surrounds us that is so common, even in its occasional unexpectedness, that we don't pay attention to it. And I'm not talking about the "magic of life" or the "magic of our senses" or any other metaphor for the wonderment we can find in life.

Here are some examples. I'm about to say something, and someone else says the same thing before me. I'm thinking of a friend and she calls unexpectedly. I need to see someone and I accidentally run into that person in a store. I need money that I don't know how to get and a check arrives out of the blue in the mail from an unexpected source.

Here's a true story of magic at work. A friend of mine wanted to buy some special bells for her mother but could not find them anywhere. One afternoon she phoned a friend but accidentally dialed the wrong number. The person at the other end turned out to be the clerk in a gift store she had never heard of. More importantly, this store turned out to be the sole importers in the whole city of these special bells.

We call these kinds of events synchronicities, manifestations, good luck, God's hand, or coincidences.

The Flame of Incarnation

We see the way people long married can complete each other's sentences, and we talk about them "being in resonance."

What all these kinds of events and experiences have in common is that something intangible—a thought, a desire, an intent—is having an effect upon something tangible. The immaterial and invisible is affecting the material and the visible. For example, one day I had to give a lecture in the city at a place that is notorious for having very limited parking as one has to park on busy city streets. It was raining, and I was not anticipating a long walk from wherever I could park back to the lecture hall. So I visualized an empty parking place right in front of the hall. When I got there, though, all the parking spaces were full, but on a hunch, I went around the block. Nothing was available, but as I came in view of the lecture hall again, a car pulled out right where I had visualized my parking place. I was able to park conveniently right in front of the hall. An invisible, intangible thought in my head had a visible, tangible consequence.

We can call this coincidence, but it happens time and again in everyone's life in one way or another. Our thoughts, feelings, intents, desires, wishes, fears, and hopes have a way of manifesting, the invisible world becoming visible.

The evidence is that life responds to us; it configures to our inner nature, to our thoughts, feelings, and spirit. This is real magic.

Why does it do this? How does it happen? What makes this magic work and create a response? Over the centuries, people have come up with different theories: the law of attraction, or the power of thought, of imagination, or of the will. All of these undoubtedly contribute and are part of this magic. At the same time, we all have examples of when they don't work, of when we thought positively about something and it did not happen or wasn't attracted or when our will or imagination did not bring about the result we wished.

The point then is not that there is no magic but that it operates more holistically than we may have thought. It isn't just the law of attraction or the power of thought or the use of the imagination. Other things may be involved, at least some of the time. And if you think about it, this makes sense. Life responds to us as whole beings, not just as thinking beings or feeling beings or imagining beings. What evokes a response at a given moment may be a mystery; we may have to do some attentive observation and experimentation to gain clues about what works for us and what doesn't. Each of us may come to this magic uniquely, based on our particular individuality; what works for someone else may not work for us because we are different people. But what is certain is that life will and does configure to us. It does respond. Who we are affects and shapes the world we experience. We are the makers and unmakers of worlds. This is everyday magic.

Experiment with this. Try it out. It may not for you be as straight-forward as thinking, "I want that new car," and it will appear. How magic works for you may operate differently based on your unique relationship with life, the way your interiority and inner nature relates and configures to the world and vice versa. But your magic will work for you and is working all the time. Be a scientist of your own invisible world and investigate to find out how.

The Flame of Incarnation

The first step into using your magic may be the same for everyone. I believe it is. It consists of simply acknowledging to oneself, "I am not a muggle. I am a magician."

No Muggles Here (Part 2)!

In part 1, I said that we are all magic-users, not, to use J.K. Rowling's term for ordinary mortals in her Harry Potter books, "muggles." I use the term "magic" here not in any metaphorical sense or as a way of expressing the wonderment of life, but as a statement of fact. Magic describes a way of relating to life, and it's a relationship we all have and express.

If I believe that the world is only what I can see, touch, hear, smell, or taste and that the appearances of things are the sum total of reality, then this magic won't make any sense. But it will still operate. I cannot avoid being a magic-user, though I can be an unmindful, unaware one.

A usual (though not the only) way magic is defined in the Western esoteric traditions, is as the shaping of events in the physical world in accordance with the will, imagination, thoughts, and feelings of the magician. Other definitions may include partnering with beings and forces of the spiritual worlds, that is, the use of inner allies.

Both these definitions assume the existence of an "inner world," a world of life and energy existing behind the appearance and surface of things. This is a world our senses cannot directly reveal. Actually, we experience exactly such a world everyday in our thoughts, our feelings, and our spiritual experiences. Magic is based on the simple idea that this world within ourselves is connected to and in fact part of an energy field that is part of the world around us. In effect, like amphibians, we live in two worlds, one that is revealed through our senses and which we can thus call a "sensible" world and one that is revealed through means other than our senses and thus could be called "supersensible."

Magic can be nothing more or less than the result of the relationship between these two worlds, a relationship we all have. This relationship can be relatively unconscious and automatic, one to which we give little thought or practice, or it can be the focus of our attention, one that we work on to develop skills and capacities to make it conscious and deliberate. Most of what we call "magical training" is designed to do the latter, and it doesn't have to take place in any kind of esoteric or occult setting. Courses in positive thinking, in motivation, in coaching, in advertising and marketing, all deal with ways of enhancing the power of our attitudes, beliefs, will, thoughts, and feelings to affect not only our own lives but outcomes in the world around us.

It works because we are all interconnected. The inner world possesses a "Commons," just like the commons of old New England villages, a shared space that all within the village can use and participate in. We each have our "private homes," our bubbles of sovereignty and subjective identity that are unique to each of us, but these radiate into, and receive from, and participate in the "energy commons" of which we are all a part. We are individualized but not isolated.

The participatory nature of this common energy world we all share gives us great power to affect the world around us, beyond the physical actions we may take. It's what truly makes us magicians and not muggles. My thoughts and feelings about another person don't necessarily remain locked up in my own head, for instance, but can become part of a local energy commons that that person shares; they can be taken by that person into his or her individual energy field and have an effect. Depending on the nature of my thoughts and feelings and upon the strength of the other person's sense of sovereignty and well-being, this could have a positive or a negative affect.

The invisible, supersensible energy world and the visible, sensible physical world are deeply intertwined and are reflections of each other. One is not necessarily the product of the other; nor are they completely hierarchically related. Each affects the other in an ecology of mutual co-creativity. For this reason the nature of our magic is both physical and non-physical. But when magic works, when synchronicities occur, when manifestation happens, when outer things change because of inner changes we've made, it's because a shift in the inner energy world has very likely caused a corresponding shift in the outer visible world. And the reverse is true, that outer changes can cause changes and shifts in supersensible energy conditions.

I am a fairly good natural singer. I can carry a tune, and people don't run screaming from the room or cover their ears when I sing. I have a friend, though, who is a trained opera singer, a soprano, and the power and range of her voice, as well as its effect on those who hear it, is amazing. My singing is like hers only in the fact that we both open our mouths to let sound come out.

We are all magic-users; we are all part of the supersensible Commons and participate in that

No Muggles Here!

Commons in ways that affect our world. But we are not all trained magicians, with developed skills of imagination, will, attunement, and lovingness. There are many systems of training that a person can engage with to develop the skills and capacities that work with this innate relationship we all have. Lorian offers in its classes one kind of training.

However, a trained magician in the sense I'm using the term may not know any esoteric or occult knowledge but simply have a dedicated and practical sense of participating in a loving, imaginative, and disciplined way in the world around him or her. Some of the best magic-users and manifestors I know, for instance, wouldn't know an occult lodge from a movie theater and have never heard of any Mystery or esoteric tradition. But they can shape the world around them in loving and blessing-filled ways for the benefit of all who come into their sphere of influence, empowering others to recognize the richness and power of their own individuality. In their presence, the Commons we all share blooms with possibilities and an invitation to success.

What better magic is there than that?

Language

The other day I heard a woman say, "I have to get rid of my ego." She said it in much the same way that President Bush says we have to get rid of terrorists. In her life, she is a loving, inclusive person, dedicated to spiritual development. Given her general orientation towards creating wholeness around her, I wondered why she didn't say, "There is that in me that gets in my way of being as loving and free as I would like. I need to understand why this is so and what this is. Perhaps I can discover how to partner with it to create wholeness within me."

However, like many of us, her language of spirituality tends towards words and images better suited for a military campaign. We learn this from our culture. Thus, she talks about "overcoming" and "defeating" the parts of her she dislikes or has been told are bad for her. She "surrenders" to spirit as if it were an invading army

Language

before whom she must wave a white flag. Dedicated to a holistic outlook in her work and relationships, she abandons it in favor of a "divide and conquer" mentality when it comes to herself and her own spirituality.

This is unfortunate. Language shapes how we think and how we act. It also influences what we think is possible. If I think of myself as divided into good and bad parts, "friends" and "enemies," and of inner work as a battle to protect the former and get rid of or destroy the latter, then I make myself a divided being, one whose energy is consumed by inner conflict. Spiritual progress becomes seen as a series of conquests over myself. But who is the victor and who the defeated?

Here's another example. Many years ago I heard a lecturer say that the relationship of the soul to the personality and body was like that of a driver to a car. This is certainly a compelling image and a common one. It draws its power from its simplicity; it is metaphorically appealing. On the other hand, it also has the effect of dividing us into at least two parts, soul and personality or spirit and body and making one subordinate to the other. After all, a car is an unthinking thing that we use, not a partner or part of our wholeness. If this is the basis of our thinking about ourselves, then it creates a foundation for the kind of inner conflict I mentioned above.

Let's call this the language of separation. It's pervasive throughout human culture. It is the language of "us" vs. "them," at the root of so much violence and suffering in our world today, and not just between people. It colors much of our thinking about our relationship to the environment was well. Not that all separative language and thinking is bad. There are times when the ability to draw clear distinctions and boundaries is important.

The Flame of Incarnation

To say that all separative thinking is wrong is itself an example of separative thinking. But there is no doubt that when such language and thinking are carried to an extreme and are not balanced by equally compelling images of our unity and connectedness, we end up with horrors like the Holocaust.

When I began my work as a spiritual teacher in 1965, I also began an association with a group of inner beings who ever since have been my colleagues. They are part of a much larger attempt within the spiritual worlds to give us a new language, one more in keeping with the needs of the world that is emerging. I remember my principle mentor at that time, a being whom I called "John," saying that the way human beings thought and spoke about themselves and spirit was itself a barrier to closer collaboration and co-creation between the physical and non-physical worlds. "You either don't believe in us or you believe too much in us, putting us on a pedestal and diminishing yourselves in the process," John said. "We seek partnership, but partnership cannot be based on one side telling the other what to do or the other submitting because it feels unworthy and unspiritual." We had a good language for discernment and separation, but we didn't have a good language for connectedness and wholeness.

This began to change in the Sixties and Seventies. Science, mathematics, and environmental research began giving us a new language to talk about ourselves and the world around us. It is a language of concepts like "holism," "systems," "interconnectedness," "interdependency," and "ecology." It is a language that sees ourselves and the world as emergent wholes.

My friend the cultural historian and poet, William

Irwin Thompson, calls the holistic thinking that understands and uses such a language a "Gaian way of knowing." It represents a significant shift in the perspectives and attitudes that prevail in our civilization, even in civilization in general. Though there have been societies in the past that have certainly honored nature and the planet, we have not had a culture that sees humanity and the world as spiritual and physical co-creators, partners, and collaborators in shaping wholeness. We have not had a civilization that teaches us to "think like a planet," which is to say, in systemic, holistic and ecological ways. To imagine the possibility that such a civilization can develop and that we can be agents of its emergence and actually begin creating it is the calling of our time.

This is so because there is no question that the language of division is insufficient as we confront planetary challenges such as climate change and a global economy, terrorism and war. We need a language of wholeness. We need a language for holopoiesis, the art of "wholeness-making."

What has been interesting to me is to see where this language has been emerging and where it lagged. Over the past thirty years, some of the most pioneering thinking and experimentation in what might be called 'Gaian consciousness" has been in business, economics, in organizational development and new theories of governance, as well as in the sciences, particularly biology, ecology and systems theory. For some examples, see the books of Harrison Owen on Open Space Technology (one of many websites is www.openspaceworld.com), Margaret Wheatley's classic book Leadership and the New Science (www.

margaretwheatley.com), the techniques of non-violent communication taught by Marshall Rosenberg (www.cnvc.org), Arnold Mindell's process psychology (www.aamindell.net), or Mark Satin's political blog on the Radical Middle (www.radicalmiddle.com). Where, it seems to me, it has been slowest to take hold is in the spiritual field (a notable exception to this has been the work of William Bloom—check out his website, www.williambloom.com or his book Soulutions.)

It's not that concepts of wholeness aren't found in spiritual teachings and traditions; they are. But it's more common, I think, to find ideas of unity than of wholeness. These are not identical concepts, and the two can be turned against each other in curious ways. Thus the woman I mentioned at the beginning felt that to achieve a state of unity, she had to become less whole, dividing herself into bits, getting rid of some while keeping the others. What she lacked was a way of thinking and speaking about herself as a whole being. Her spiritual language didn't give her tools for holopoiesis.

We need such tools. It is hard to be agents of creating wholeness in the world if we cannot create it in ourselves, and it's hard to create it in ourselves if we believe that it's fundamentally lacking in us, that the very nature of who and what we are arises from separation and division. Yet when we speak of our incarnations as journeys away from God and spirit, when we think of life as a kind of exile from our real home, when we think of ourselves as divided into souls and personalities, when we think of the physical world as simply an illusion from which we must awaken, we may well be speaking (and thinking) in a language of separation rather than connection and wholeness-making.

Language

It was for this reason, I believe, that a number of years ago the inner beings with whom I work suggested I focus my attention on incarnation itself. What I call incarnational spirituality has grown out of that research, which is ongoing. I've gained numerous insights in this process, but one of the most important has been to see incarnation itself as an act of wholeness-making.

Various traditions and schools of spirituality identify different reasons why we may come to this world: to work out past karma, to learn lessons, to evolve, to perform some specific task, and so on. But deeper than any of these reasons, we are gifts of love to enhance the connections between the physical and non-physical dimensions and to build the wholeness of the earth.

We cannot build wholeness if we do not feel whole within ourselves, but we cannot feel whole in ourselves if we cannot speak of who we are in a language of connection and wholeness. It's this language that is striving to develop and unfold in our midst. It's not an easy birth, even when we desire it, for we have spoken for so long in languages of separation and conflict that they insinuate themselves into our thinking even when we are talking about wholeness. "My ego is the source of my problems; I must get rid of it to be whole." But once we get rid of it—if we can get rid of it—then what takes its place? What new part of ourselves shall we identify as the new culprit and the next target for removal? How much self-division and self-amputation does wholeness demand? The correct answer is none at all, but to understand that, we must learn to see, to think, and to speak in a different way, in the language of Gaia rather than the language of a fragmented—and fragmenting—humanity.

The Flame of Incarnation

The elements of this language are emerging. This is the most exciting thing about our time. It is a language that has the power to create a new world because it can enable us to see a new us. Incarnational spirituality is part of this language, the part that focuses on incarnation, self, sovereignty, generativity, relationships and even boundaries as elements and acts of wholeness-making. But other parts are emerging as well, in holistic spirituality itself and in science, business, politics, indeed in many walks of life as individuals respond to the possibilities of a new world and a new vision.

Is this possible? Can we learn a new language to heal our world and heal ourselves? I believe so. It's why I do what I do and teach what I teach. It's why Lorian exists. More importantly, I believe it's why we're all here, to make this shift. The language of wholeness may be new in some ways but in reality it is our native tongue. It may not be a matter of learning something new but of remembering something basic within us, the deep language of our souls, the grammar of love and the vocabulary of being human.

Let's explore more fully what a new language of wholeness-making might sound like in the context of dealing with ego. If "ego" is something we need to confront, then how might we do so in a holistic and not a separative way?

Ego

Earlier in my essay on Language, I talked about the need for a language of holopoiesis or "wholeness-making," and said I would explore more fully what such a language might sound like in the context of dealing with ego. If "ego" is something we need to confront, then how might we do so in a holistic and not a separative way?

The word ego has different meanings depending on how it's used and who's using it. It comes from a Latin root meaning simply "self" or the quality of "I-ness." In psychology it's used to describe certain mental functions that are a necessary element of healthy functioning and mental wellbeing. In some esoteric teachings, the ego is the personality, the instrumentality of incarnation and individuation. But in other philosophies it's used to mean the part of us that divides, separates, deceives, seeks control, and basically acts in unspiritual and nasty ways. It's our "false self," our "little self," our "selfish self," the part that is self-absorbed and wants its own way at the expense of others, the bastion of all things negative about us and our lives, rooted in fear and illusion.

Thus, depending on how we define it, ego is either an essential part of our humanness and our identity, necessary for our psychological and spiritual wellbeing and development, or it's the opposite, an impediment to our growth and well being or even worse, a source of the evils that beset humanity.

Behind the idea of ego is an attempt to understand ourselves and why we behave the way we do. And there is also the sentiment, comforting in its simplicity, that there is a single origin for the ills that we do or which others have done to us. Surely there is some flawed part which we can either remove or correct and then everything will be fine.

But what if, as the holistic worldview suggests, things are more complex than that?

Let's consider the game of golf.

Golf is a simple sport to describe. You are trying to knock a small ball into a hole in the ground with a club in the shortest number of strokes from a starting point several hundred yards away. Golf would be a simple sport, and a rather boring one, if all one had to do was swing a club and hit a ball. But any golfer knows that to do this well enough to get a competitive score requires skill in how the body moves and interacts with its environment. The key to playing successfully is your stroke, the way in which you hit the ball in order to control where it goes.

This stroke is a complex interaction between vision,

posture, musculature, the nature of the club, how you hold the club, the position of the ball, terrain, moisture, wind conditions, ambience such as noise, and your mental and emotional state. The success of a stroke in getting the ball just where the golfer desires it to go depends on how skillfully the golfer weaves these elements together into a wholeness. A whole industry has developed around the understanding and development of the stroke and its variations depending on the position of the ball relative to the hole and the terrain on which it's laying.

When everything comes together, you see a ball rising and falling with precision and beauty to land just where the golfer intended, perhaps even rolling into the cup for a hole-in-one. When it doesn't, well, that's when you get to visit sand traps or hunt for your ball in the rough areas to the side of the fairway. Or when you wonder where the ball went and then look down to see it still sitting on the tee, perhaps trembling a bit from the passage of the wind as your club sailed over it.

When this happens, an amateur golfer may look for excuses. He may say it's the fault of his clubs and throw them away. Or he may claim it was his eyesight or the muscles in his arm or some other single factor. And it's possible he's right. He may have chosen the wrong club for the job (no pity allowed for the guy who tries to putt with a driver or vice versa), or he may need glasses to see better. But it's far more likely that his poor results are a combination of a number of issues, such as grip, stance, posture, the kinetics of his swing, and so on. A good golf pro or teacher will address this problem by considering the person in his or her wholeness. It would be very unlikely that he would advise the duffer, "Well, your hands are gripping the club wrong, so why don't you cut them off and get rid of them."

I have a similar experience in writing. Sometimes I work a paragraph over and over trying to find just the right way to say what I want. I've been known to rewrite a single chapter in a book as many as twenty times before I'm satisfied. And sometimes I get into a flow—in the writer's zone—and the words just come. Everything flows together and I hit a "chapter-in-one." But when this doesn't happen (which is most of the time!), I don't think, "Well, there's an evil part of me that keeps putting wrong words in my head." It would be nice if that were true because that would make correcting the situation easier, but in fact, the reasons why my writing may not come together at a particular time are numerous and complex, including physical and mental fatigue, lack of proper vocabulary for the task, distractions in the environment (I'd rather be outside in the sunshine!), lack of clarity in my ideas, and so on.

In both cases, what we're talking about is skill, a person's skill as a golfer and my skill as a writer, and both are made up of complex and dynamical relationships between a number of factors.

A holistic view sees our interactions with life as a skill as well. When things go well, it's like finding the right words or hitting the perfect stroke. And when they don't, well, we've swung and missed, and there are probably a number of reasons for that, not one evil source within us called "the ego." Indeed, a focus on the ego (or anything else) as the origin of our problems lessens the chance that we will actually understand the complexity of the situation and the skills (or lack of them) that are involved. If I say my lousy golf score is due to my clubs, chances are I'll never improve for I'll never look at all the other physical, psychological and environmental factors that go into a good stroke.

But it's simpler and entails less responsibility for me to just throw out my old clubs and buy new ones. Who cares if my game never really improves? Golf for me will become a sport of continually buying and trying out new clubs hoping to find the perfect driver, the perfect irons and the perfect putter.

In a similar way, I've met people for whom spirituality consists of "dealing with their ego" but who remain blind to the lack of skill in their overall interpersonal dealings and attitudes that continue to create problems for them. They are fixated on one part of them being wrong or broken and if they get rid of it or fix it, all will be well. And once they've fixed or gotten rid of whatever it is, then, like the golfer who blames his clubs, they find some other part of them to blame for their problems. Then it's time for more fixing! More getting rid of!

Which brings us back to the original question. In a holistic perspective, how does one deal with ego?

Not by considering it a separate part, nor by blaming it (or any other single element in our lives) for our problems. We see ourselves as a whole system, just as a great golfer sees himself as a whole being interacting with a whole environment. And we think of our interactions with life as a skill that needs attention and practice. Finding the dynamic balance between meeting our own needs, the needs of others, the needs of the environment in which we find ourselves, and the needs of the larger energy and spiritual contexts of which we are a part is like learning to dance or hit a golf ball or write well or figure skating on ice. It is a skill and one that

Ego

includes configuring to the particulars of the moment. The genius of a professional golfer is that he or she can adapt to the changing environment. If his stroke is off and the ball doesn't go where he wants, he doesn't say, "Oh, that was a bad swing." He'll be more precise. "This was a bad swing because…" and he'll mentally review what happened in that particular moment under those particular conditions.

Likewise, for me to say, "Oh, that was my ego," effectively tells me nothing that will help me improve my skill of living. What does "ego" mean in this moment under these conditions in this situation? Does it really mean I was selfish and self-centered? Then I should say, "Oh, I was acting selfishly because my attention and desire were on my needs and no one else's." That's a very specific statement that I can then act upon to improve my skill. It tells me what I can do to learn. Instead of telling myself, "I need to get rid of my ego," I can say, "I need to pay more attention to others in this situation and not worry so much about having my own needs met."

Or maybe I was fearful. Instead of saying that fear is an ego condition, I can examine the fear. Was it terror? Was it fear? Was it anxiety? What kind of fear was it? Where did it come from? Some fears give me valuable survival information and are based on real threats in the environment. Was it that kind of fear? Or was it a groundless anxiety based on a past memory or perhaps on psychically picking up fearful energies in my environment? And wherever the fear came from, how did it make me react? Did I feel constricted in my energy? Did I panic? Did I focus on myself to the exclusion of others? What specifically happened? What was the nature of my "swing" that led me to hit one into that relational sand trap?

Being specific changes the nature of the event from one of focusing on a postulated evil, false, or lesser part of me to focusing upon my actions and behavior as elements that demonstrated more or less skill in relationship and awareness. I become less blaming of myself and others and more aware of my capacity to improve my skill. This opens the door to learning.

Perhaps the single greatest difference in holopoietic language is that I simply refuse to chop myself up into pieces in how I describe and talk about myself. Instead of saying, "It was my ego," I say simply, "It was me. The whole me, not a part of me. I am responsible as a whole being for what happened. I will not honor that responsibility or that wholeness simply by cutting something out and getting rid of it."

The holistic view is that life is about practice, not surgery.

The Haggled Self

When I was six, my father's work took our family to Morocco where we lived for the next six years. I had many memorable experiences in that country but one that I particularly remember was watching Dad sit down in a store in the native market or souk and haggle. Being fluent in Arabic and being willing to haggle gave him an advantage right at the start, for most Americans were seen as naïve and even stupid for their readiness to pay whatever price the merchant first asked and their unwillingness to take the time to negotiate. For us, commerce was an economic transaction, the buying and selling of goods; for the Moroccan it was a social transaction. The haggling wasn't really about getting a good bargain. It was about forming a relationship and getting to know another person. It was a game of wits, but if played properly, both sides won and both were enriched beyond the exchange of currency and items.

The Haggled Self

I didn't often go with Dad when he ventured into the souks to do his haggling. A single purchase could easily take an hour or more as mint tea was brought out and served and my father and the merchant would converse about many things quite apart from buying the rug, the tray, the tea set, or whatever had caught Dad's fancy. As the conversation was in Arabic, which I did not speak, I would get impatient with the process. But sometimes, if Dad knew the merchant, he would take me along and I would be served treats and given interesting things to look at while the grownups conducted their business.

I was reminded of this the other day when I heard someone talking about his "True Self." By this he meant the spiritual part of himself, whatever that might be, with the implication that his personality was a false self. Surprisingly, what popped into my mind was the thought that in haggling, nothing has a true price. The price emerges from the relationship in the moment.

At first, I wondered why this thought had been prompted by the man's comments about his "True Self." So I began thinking about haggling. In our culture when we go to a store and ask what something costs, we're shown a price tag. I pick up a book, for instance, and right on the cover the price is printed: "$7.99" or "$14.99" or whatever it may be. The value is established, (even if it's called the "Manufacturer's Suggested Retail Price) as if it's an intrinsic part of the item.

But when we haggle over an item, it doesn't have an intrinsic price tag. It may have an intrinsic worth based on the materials it contains, which may be added to by subjective factors such as the time and energy spent in creating it. But it doesn't have a monetary value. That value emerges from our negotiations and can be based on a number of factors unrelated to the item itself. I may be feeling generous, so I'm willing to practically give you the item, or I may be feeling fearful and greedy, in which case I want to get as much money from you as I can. You bring your own needs, feelings, and perceptions to the table. From all of this mix, a price eventually emerges. Now we know what this item is worth, though it is a value unique to this moment and this exchange. Had we haggled over it yesterday or were we to haggle over it tomorrow, a different price might have been established.

So in this sense, the item has no "true price." In haggling, which might be termed "relationship economics," the price arises from all the factors that go into the interaction.

But this is not as arbitrary as it may seem. There is a cost to the item and a value to the materials from which it's made as well as the craftsmanship, time, and energy of manufacture. The merchant brings certain expenses and resources to the table. He has needs to be met. Likewise, my father did not have a bottomless purse. He had financial resources he could draw on, but they certainly weren't unlimited. The haggling relationship took place within definite boundaries. To go beyond those boundaries, to suggest a price that was unreasonably high or low, was to disrespect the relationship and the haggling process.

So even though there was no "true price," there were truths that were brought to the enterprise. My father, the merchant, and the item each brought the truth of their individual conditions and identities. For instance, the fact that Dad spoke Arabic and was willing to haggle and observe the social customs was a truth that made the merchant more favorably inclined towards him and set the beginning offer lower than it might have been otherwise.

Thinking of this, I realize that I don't have a sense of having a "True Self" (nor, for that matter, a "false self" either). I have a sense of different levels and layers of Self, but all of them seem true to me—and all of them emerge in some way out of relationship with other forces and with a large context. They are all "haggled" selves, or to put it more simply, I am a haggled self. (Sometimes a haggard one as well, but that's a different story!)

I like that image. It doesn't mean that I have no value, identity, or meaning but rather that my identity is part of a participatory, co-creative, co-incarnational process. The universe has not set a price on me; I'm free to determine that price—that worth—myself in dialog with the cosmos.

I understand what the gentleman who spoke of his "True Self" was getting at. We all have a sense that there is some part of us that is not a product simply of the whims and fortunes of fate, that does not change day by day, and that provides a source of constancy and coherency, a sense of continuity and integrity. But in the haggling metaphor, that represents to me what I might call my "resource self," the resources I bring to the daily negotiations of life, just as my father brought certain financial resources to the merchant's bargaining table. These are resources of spirit, wisdom, energy, soul, sacredness which I can draw upon. They are part of my truth, the truth I bring to the daily process. The world brings its own truths and its own resources.

But these are not unchanging. If we hit a bad financial patch, Dad would not shop at all in the souks or would approach his haggling from a much more restricted position; if we were flush, then he went with more abundant resources. But the resources he had didn't affect the process of the haggling itself. They shaped the relationship but were not at the core of it. That core was the honor and respect that Dad and the merchant paid to each other as partners in a social enterprise. Even if no sale was made at all, they still enjoyed each other and had a good time. There was a value to the process itself. And part of that process is the truth each participant brings to it.

I think what bothered me about the idea of a "True Self," in the sense that the gentleman was using it, was the implication that all other levels and experiences of Self were false. This seemed like saying we each carry an ultimate inner "price tag" that determines who we are independent of the world and of others, a "Manufacturer's Suggested Retail Price" of the soul stamped on us when we leave the factory, and that all other possible identities are false. These other identities might undervalue or overvalue us, but whether they are false or not depends on what the world is willing to offer and what we're willing to accept.

For me, our True Self is our capacity to engage with the world in a way that the greatest possible value and result for all of us can emerge through our participation and relationships with life. It's not so much the part of us that is eternal and unchanging but the part of us that really knows how to haggle.

The Sweet Spot

My wife plays African drums. In drumming, she tells me, you try to hit the sweet spot, the place on the drum where you get the best tone for the stroke you're making and the sound you want to produce. When the sweet spot is struck, there is a depth and resonance to the note that is unmistakable.

We use the phrase "sweet spot" in other situations, too, to indicate that moment or place where all elements come together to produce an optimal expression for whatever the intent may be.

I think we each have a personal sweet spot as well. It's the state of mind in which we experience the most joy and satisfaction in being ourselves. And from that place of pleasure and joy in being ourselves, energy arises to flow out into our day bringing with it the depth and resonance of our own beingness, bringing with it blessing.

The Sweet Spot

Sometimes I think spirituality is all about finding and hitting that sweet spot. Indeed, part of my personal spiritual practice is to find that sweet spot and hit it as often and consistently as I can. When I do, it's as if my life and energy in that moment become a full, rounded "note." I feel more spacious and connected, and it's easier for me to pay attention to what's happening around me in a spirit of love and blessing.

So how do you find your "sweet spot?"

Well, there's a bit of exploration involved. The sweet spot on a drum depends on a number of factors such as how the drum is constructed, the materials that are used, especially for the drumhead, the type of stroke the drummer is making, weather conditions that affect temperature and moisture in the air, and so on. It's unique for each drum, though there are commonalities as well. A drummer has to get to know her instrument and herself as well as a drummer. But when you hit it, you know it. You can feel the response of the drum as it "thrums" beneath your hand (I do some occasional drumming, too, though nowhere near as much as my wife), and you can feel the note expanding out into the universe. As I said, it's unmistakable.

With your own sweet spot, you're looking for a thought or feeling in the moment that brings you joy in being who you are. Maybe for many people, *joy* is too strong a word; I don't mean by it the kind of ecstasy that sends you whooping and dancing out into the street. But I don't mean mere happiness, either. I mean a sense of satisfaction and pleasure at being in your own company, a sense of exhilaration at being *you* in the world as you are right at this moment.

The sweet spot is not the same as a feeling of

confidence or self-esteem. It is certainly not a narcissistic indulgency of self-admiration. Confidence and self-esteem can add to it; they are like structural conditions of the drum, but they are not themselves the sweet spot. Sometimes, in fact, the sweet spot is an oasis of momentary joy and connectedness in a desert of self-judgment and criticism, self-doubt and angst. It is not dependent on being a "positive thinker" or even on "loving yourself," although the latter certainly doesn't hurt and, like self-esteem, can be an important structural component of how you construct the drum of your life.

I can find my sweet spot at times by simply taking a moment to appreciate myself, flaws and all. But paradoxically, I find my sweet spot most easily and readily when I don't think about myself at all, at least not in a self-reflective way or being the center of my attention.

A drum has a sweet spot but in a way it's not a part of the drum in the same way that the drumhead is or the frame is. A drum maker doesn't have "sweet spots" stored in her studio waiting to be attached to a new drum. The sweet spot emerges from a convergence of factors that form a pattern which includes the drummer.

In a similar way, my sweet spot is not a spiritual or psychological part of me like my soul or my unconscious mind. It's not a "high self" or a "low self" or any kind of self, for that matter. It's something that emerges from a pattern of thoughts, feelings, and actions in the moment; it emerges, as it does with a drum, from interaction. To come into being, the sweet spot of a drum needs the stroke of the drummer, and different strokes can find different sweet spots on the same drum.

The Sweet Spot

I find my sweet spot in the moment (and it's always "in the moment") through interacting with my world. And what is that interaction? It's invariably one of appreciation and gratitude, wonder and delight; they are part of the stroke that brings out my sweet spot.

Here's are some examples:

I wake up in the morning and take a few minutes not to meditate but to appreciate the world I'm waking up to and, for that matter, appreciating the sheer fact of waking up. "Here I am again," I think to myself, "reassembled as David after a night's sleep and unconsciousness or after the very different David I am sometimes in dreams." I am aware of things about me in the dark, the furniture of the bedroom, shadowy shapes hanging in the closet. My everyday mind has not yet fully taken hold, so I can see these things as if for the first time, with no need to give them names but just appreciating their presence, appreciating that I can see them, appreciating that we're in the world together in the stillness of the morning. Rather than collapsing immediately into my everyday routines, I am stretched like a drumhead from myself to the things around me, feeling the connections. And in that sense of connectedness, I hit a sweet spot. I feel the sheer wonder of being alive. I feel a joy just at being this particular point of consciousness the world calls "David," not because of anything David is or has done or is doing but simply because I'm present in the world and thus the world and I can experience each other. Who knows what possibilities may unfold from this? What wonder! What delight! Thrummmmm! The note of my life echoes into the bedroom, into the world, and into my own heart. In that moment, I feel spacious, deep, joyous, and in love not as an emotion but as a presence.

This may not last. It doesn't have to. When my wife plays the drum, she hits it over and over again, each note adding to the next, playing the melody. Not every stroke hits the sweet spot, not every note reverberates out to infinity, but many do. And as she has become more skilled and attentive as a drummer, more and more notes come from the sweet spots she and the drum co-create.

So as I enter my day, I may lose this spacious, resonant, "thrumming" note of love and blessing. But not to worry! The world and I are still a drum together. I have more strokes in me; there are more notes to play.

The day goes on. Whenever I think of it, I can stop and appreciate something about where I am. I sit here writing this, for instance, and with part of my mind, I can appreciate the sheer wonderment of writing, of translating intangible thoughts into words and images, of joining with you hopefully in a communion of meaning and experience. Wow! The wonder of language! Amazing! And here I am, using language, using my fingers, working on this incredible technology called a computer, feeling meaning bubble within me and find its way corked in words on this page for you to open, hopefully with a "pop!" of effervescence that sends the life and sparkle of that meaning bubbling up in you. Fantastic! It's another sweet spot!

Or I turn my head. Next to my desk is a book case with a number of books, and every book has a cover that's a different color or combination of colors. If I look at the books and don't try to read the writing on them but just appreciate the colors, it's like a bookshelf full of rainbows. And think of all the bubbles of meaning and insight corked within them! Oh, Sweet Spot again as I appreciate the books, the color, the writing, and the wonder of me being here, seeing them, able to read them, enjoying them.

The other evening we watched a movie called *Hogfather* based on a fantasy novel of the same name by Terry Pratchett. It's a well done and funny movie (and book, too; Pratchett is a very funny writer indeed). In it one of the main characters, Death, says something like, "I have a fondness for humanity. It's the only species that can live in a world so filled with wonder and still invent boredom!"

This is a wonderful thought. There are so many opportunities during our day to stop and feel a sense of joy just in being in such an amazing and wondrous world, so full of life and possibilities. It's nothing more complicated than a moment of appreciation, and with it an appreciation for one's presence in this world in this moment. That stroke is the one that finds the sweet spot for me.

With it comes a sense that the world is *good*. Not perfect. Not without flaws. Not without serious challenges. Not without heartache and suffering. But filled with *goodness*. And when we hit our sweet spot, we know that we are part of that goodness. In that moment, as that note of our life echoes out, we know that we are good, too.

And what do you do when you find your sweet spot? You let it resound in your heart and send it forth as blessing into the world. In that moment let the world know you appreciate yourself, that you appreciate it, and that together you are good. Feel the note of your sweet spot not only fill your body but the environment around you. Let it be a sound of love, a note of delight, a thrum of wonder and appreciation. It moves in silence, but what a silence!

Hitting your sweet spot, taking time and attention to do so, even practicing doing so like a good drummer, is a real gift you can offer our world. In a world of anxiety and fear, pain and trembling, hurt and sickness, from our sweet spot comes love, joy, spaciousness, blessing: a resounding note of connectedness and wholeness. It may only last for a moment, but the melody of the world's healing is made up of millions of such single moments woven together as countless people hit their sweet spots, some deliberately, some by accident, some unconsciously but all resounding with promise and hope. It's a gift anyone can make. You have a sweet spot no matter who you are or what you do.

If you find your sweet spot and then in the next moment you lose it, you can find it again. The drum between you and the world is always there, and you are always a drummer. If one stroke doesn't do it, you can try another.

British playwright Christopher Fry ends his play *A Sleep of Prisoners* like this: "*It takes /So many thousand years to wake/But will you wake for pity's sake?*" I'd like to close with a paraphrase:

Your sweet spot's note the world awaits,
So will you strike for pity's sake?

The Flame of Incarnation

The Incarnational Way

What a January it's been! We had wild weather, wilder economics, and the Inauguration of a charismatic and young new President of the United States that set off an explosion of joy and hope. I want to begin this David's Desk by wishing President Barack Obama and his Administration well, for their success at the monumental and historic tasks before them will be a success for all of us. Ultimately, the tasks are ours anyway. Over two hundred years ago, Abraham Lincoln appealed to the "better angels of our nature;" a little over two weeks ago, Barack Obama appealed to our ability to "choose our better history." In both our better nature and our better history lie powers of compassion, wisdom, love, and a pragmatic, can-do spirit that can transform our world for the better, but it always remains our choice to rise to those possibilities.

January is also my birth month, and as such, it's

The Incarnational Way

always been a time of reflection for me. This time I wanted to step back and take stock of what it is I'm doing—or trying to do. For nearly fifty years now I've been serving a particular vision of our human spiritual potential, a vision that came to me unexpectedly one summer as I was in that magical place between graduating high school and starting college in the fall. Eventually, the power and calling of this vision led me to leave school and my hopes of becoming a molecular biologist to take on the very uncertain and challenging but always rewarding path of being a spiritual teacher.

Sometimes in these past years, this vision has been crystal clear to me, while other times it's been cloudy and difficult to grasp. When it comes to articulating it, especially so that others can understand and benefit from it, I feel I've had both successes and failures. In recent years, I've called this vision variously "incarnational spirituality," the "incarnational way," or simply an incarnational worldview.

What is this worldview?

Fundamentally it is about our "better natures" and our capacities to choose a "better history." My colleagues in the non-physical realms, the ones who presented me with this worldview in the first place and have been my partners in its articulation and expression ever since, have a simple purpose: they want us all to live well and prosper, to paraphrase the Vulcan greeting from Star Trek, and to do so in a way that enhances the wellbeing and prosperity of all life. They wish us to live our lives on the earth in a manner that blesses us and creates a future that blesses the world. With their view of our better natures, they see us as quite capable of doing so.

They see this because to them we are spiritual beings

as fully as they are. We are not in their eyes "spiritual beings having a human experience," as if that human experience were divorced from spirit in some way; in short, we're not "down here" slumming. We are spiritual beings having an experience of spirit in a particular form that we call the physical world.

If we think of incarnation at all, we usually think of something transpersonal and spiritual inserting itself into something personal and physical. A familiar metaphor for incarnation is that our souls enter our bodies the way a driver gets into a car. But this is a flawed image both in its perception of a duality between soul and body and in its portrayal of how an incarnation takes place.

It would be more accurate to think of incarnation as akin to a chemical reaction that combines several different elements to produce a new alloy, a reaction that in the process generates energy. In incarnation the elements that come together may be thought of as energies or presences. They include the energy and intentionality of the soul, the energies of the world and of nature (which collectively I think of as the World Soul), the energies of spirit and the non-physical realms, and the energy of sacredness. The "alloy" they co-create through their relationship is an individual—you, me and everyone else. We are each a unique manifestation of this relationship which at its heart is enabled and empowered by love. Love is at the heart of every incarnation as that which brings and holds the diverse elements together so that the alloy of individuality can emerge.

Like physical chemical reactions, this spiritual "reaction" generates a unique spiritual energy, one that does not come from somewhere else but emerges from the incarnational process itself. It is a spiritual force

The Incarnational Way

and energy that emerges from our intent to be part of this physical world and the process that implements that intent. The act of incarnation itself is a dynamic relationship that makes each of us spiritually radiant, a source of spiritual energy.

Many, if not most, spiritual traditions acknowledge that there is an inner light within us and that we possess a spiritual component. This is what Lincoln referred to as the "angels of our better nature." But most would see this light and spirit as coming from somewhere else or would identify it as "the God within" or the "Divine Spark," a part of us that is separate and distinct from the physical world around us. Such a transpersonal light, spirit or energy does exist within us; in fact, it's one of the elements that is necessary for the "chemical reaction" of incarnation to take place. But the radiant energy that actually is produced by the act of incarnation is a unique spiritual force, an "angel" or a "better nature" in its own right. It doesn't come from anywhere else; it comes from the incarnational process itself. It is a product of our being here, and its generation is one of the reasons we take incarnation in the first place.

I call it our self-light. Think of a light that comes on automatically in a room when you enter it. Our self-light is a radiant, spiritual force that "comes on" when we incarnate; it manifests as our individuality. And because incarnation is a process not a onetime event, this light has the potential to develop and grow throughout our lives.

Over fifty years, since I was first introduced to the existence of this incarnational radiance and spiritual force, I have sought to understand it with the help of my non-physical allies and colleagues. While we often see such non-physical beings as radiant sources of spiritual blessing, this is precisely how they see us as well. This incarnational light that emanates from us is a vital part of the world, a gift to the cosmos; we are spiritual energy sources in the world and not just energy recipients or energy consumers.

This should not be too unusual a thought if we think about it. Our bodies take in food and convert it into the substance of those bodies, releasing biological energy in the process. We are all generating life energies all the time; why not see ourselves as generating and radiating spiritual energies as well?

What is important to this perception is that this self-light is a part of this world, a product of the act of taking on embodiment and being a physical human being. We are sources of spiritual energy because we are in the world and not because we are in some way apart from it. It is not a light or spiritual energy we bring from somewhere else. It is a spiritual force we generate by being here and making this world, this dimension, our home. It is "indigenous,' so to speak. Realizing this can be wonderfully liberating and uplifting, giving a whole new meaning and value to being human and being in a physical body.

When I had my original vision about this self-light when I was seventeen, I was told that a spiritual practice would emerge that would honor and work with this incarnational light, this spiritual radiance of our personhood. Over the years I have worked to explore and give voice to what this practice might be like. The incarnational spirituality I teach through our Lorian classes is a result of that exploration, an exploration that is ongoing and evolving.

The Incarnational Way

There are different kinds of spirituality, and each attunes to one of the important and contributing elements of the "reaction" that manifests as incarnation. The mystical path usually focuses on the spiritual experiences and qualities that come directly from the Sacred. Esoteric or magical paths focus on spiritual energies and forces that come from the non-physical worlds and from the beings within them—what I call the Second Ecology. The shamanic and earth-based spiritualities such as Wicca or Druidism work with the spiritual powers and energies coming from the land, from nature, and from life itself, as well as dealing with invisible beings.

What I think of as the "incarnational way" focuses on the spiritual power of our incarnational light, the light that "comes on" and is generated by the incarnational process itself. It is a spirituality of individuality and personhood, which are the fruits of incarnation and the mechanism for bringing this incarnational light to the world. It is this personal light that is often overlooked in the quest for transpersonal experiences and contacts. Yet it is in the understanding and cultivation of this incarnational self-light that we connect with that angel of our better nature that is most attuned to our personal wholeness and also most concerned with and able to serve the wellbeing and wholeness of the earth itself.

The incarnational way is a way dedicated to creating wholeness in all aspects of life. It could hardly be otherwise. Incarnation is an act that occurs in partnership with the sacred, with the soul, with the world and nature, and with the non-physical realms. Our self-light is not independent from these other forms of spiritual energy but integrates them in an ecology of blessing and radiance. The generative spiritual energy of incarnation is a force for wholeness in the world because it emerges itself from an act of wholeness.

In other words, the incarnational way is one of blessing ourselves but also blessing the life we all share as part of this world. Incarnation is about partnership and relationship.

Further, because it is indigenous to this world, it can usually make connections with earthly matters and produce an effect of blessing more efficiently and gracefully than can a transpersonal or transcendent force which may be too subtle to be readily perceived or felt. It has certainly been true in my experience in working with people for many years that where a person may have a challenge in connecting with the transpersonal or transcendent forces in their lives, he or she can more readily connect with the spiritual energies that emerge from his or her own personhood and incarnation once they grasp that such energies exist.

There are important implications to this for all kinds of subtle energy work such as energy hygiene, manifestation, prayer, and the emerging field of subtle activism. It has been my work and the work of Lorian to explore and develop these implications to find additional ways in which we may serve the planetary needs of our time.

The incarnational way affirms that we have "better natures" and that they exist in us not simply because there is something in us that is "higher" and "more spiritual" than the world around us but because there is a light in us that is part of the world and at home in the world, a product of our loving choice and act to be here in this world. As incarnate persons possessing and generating an incarnational light, we are ourselves the physical angels who create these better natures. If we understand this, we discover we have an innate spiritual resource to tap that is completely natural and indigenous to us as citizens of the earth. And when we tap it, we can become the blessing from which a better history, a better future, can emerge.

The Flame of Incarnation

About the Publisher

Lorian Press is a private, for profit business which publishes works approved by the Lorian Association. Current titles by David Spangler and others can be found on the Lorian website www.lorian.org.

The Lorian Association is a not-for-profit educational organization. Its work is to help people bring the joy, healing, and blessing of their personal spirituality into their everyday lives. This spirituality unfolds out of their unique lives and relationships to Spirit, by whatever name or in whatever form that Spirit is recognized.

For more information, go to www.lorian.org, email info@lorian.org, or write to:

The Lorian Association
P.O. Box 1368
Issaquah, WA 98027